Catt,
Thanks for letting me teach the hockey classes... it opened up a new world!

Kim Interdonato

HEELS & HOCKEY SKATES Woman POWER Skater
Copyright © 2018 Kim Interdonato. All rights reserved.

No part of this book may be used or reproduced in any manner whatsoever without written permission, except in the case of brief quotations embodied in critical articles and reviews. For more information, e-mail all inquiries to info@mindstirmedia.com.

Published by Mindstir Media LLC
45 Lafayette Rd. Suite 181 | North Hampton, NH 03862 | USA
1.800.767.0531 | www.mindstirmedia.com

Printed in the United States of America
ISBN-13: 978-0-9998275-0-5
Library of Congress Control Number: 2018931220

CONTENTS

Dedication: 7

The Beginning 9

First Lesson 13

No Pain, No Gain 16

Appearance 19

A Man's World 22

Overcoming Obstacles 26

Hockey Smell 29

Hockey Mom 32

Money, Money, Money 35

Women in Power 38

Styling 42

Testimonials 46

Photo Gallery 53

Never Give Up 57

DEDICATION:

To my mom for encouraging me to write a book about women in power skating.

To my dad, who told me simply, "You have a choice to be happy or sad in life." Thanks, Dad. I chose to be happy.

To my son Luke, follow your dreams, and work hard, and it will be the most rewarding lesson I could ever teach you.

To my Florida family, family and loyal friends who have been so supportive with all the kind words.

To all my students whom I was blessed to teach over the years. I hope I have enriched and enhanced your lives much as you have mine. Never give up on being your best.

To my Rinx Family, thank you for letting me do the job I cherish for so many years!

The Beginning

Wine snobs do not pair fish with red wine. A car enthusiast would not compare a Ferrari to a Fiat. And you would never pair high heels with hockey skates—unless you were a female power skating instructor like myself.

It is not the most common job for a shoe-loving girl. Off my hockey skates, I love to wear my high heels when I go shopping, out to a restaurant, and to work. I enjoy sporting the latest fashion in shoe wear. I even wrote a book about shoes! The only thing better than shoes is shoes on sale!

Wearing my heels makes me feel confident and attractive. I like the way they accent my legs. My years of skating have given me muscular legs. I like the extra height that I have gotten used to from being up on hockey skates.

When other women walk by, I have to sneak a peek. This is in no way judgemental, but to admire her shoe choice. Shoes on men and woman are one of the things I notice first. I can appreciate a nice shoe on men, women, and children.

I think I like to keep my feet looking good in pretty shoes because they are working in hockey skates every day.

When meeting someone for the first time, the question that inevitably comes up is, what do you do for a living? When I tell them I am a hockey instructor, I get mixed reactions. Some people are very curious, and some think it is cool, while other people think I am lying or they laugh in disbelief. So from time to time, I would say I am a rocket scientist, and they look and me with a head tilt like it was more believable to them than my being a hockey instructor.

I love to play dress up and prance around in high heels off the skating rink. The years of skating have helped with the balance in those high heels . . . except for the time I was walking down the steps at a popular restaurant in New Orleans. I was wearing a beautiful outfit and great heels. You know that feeling you get when you know you look good? Well, that was it for me. That night about five handsome men were drinking at the bar at the end of the steps. I took one bad step and down I went. I slid down the steps as if I was sleigh-riding without a sled, popping off my butt, slamming down onto every agonizing step. It was not pretty, but I did have a lot of guys help me up. Of course, none of them asked the clumsy girl for her number. It happened when I first walked in and was sober. They assumed I was drinking heavily, so I did not even get a sympathy drink. I was definitely not about to engage a conversation with any of them and tell them I was a professional skater. I had a better shot with the rocket scientist gig.

As a young girl growing up in the 1970s, there were only a handful of girls who played hockey. I was not one of them. I started out as a figure skater at a local rink when I was ten years old. I was an average skater. I did little competitions and held my own. Back then not everyone got a "participation trophy." I seemed to miss the podium often. My trophy shelf was a little empty. I never wanted to give up, though. It just made me work harder. I had a passion for skating.

It was not the fancy dresses—I never liked to wear them. It was not the artistry—I was a gangly, skinny kid with a very bad perm. As a kid, I hated the cold and still do to this day. Why would I want to skate?

I think all skaters have a defining moment when we really want to learn to skate. For me, it was when I went to my first ice show at about nine years old. I saw a woman doing a fast scratch spin. As she was doing the spin, I could see she was wearing a harness-type contraption around her and then she started levitating over the ice. It was so cool! I turned to my mother and said, "I want to do that someday." She patronized me and said sure, maybe someday. I sat there in amazement, thinking how neat would it be to trade places with that girl. To this day, I do not remember anything thing else from that performance but the spinning girl on ice skates.

After a year or so of begging, I finally had my first lesson at age ten. It did not go as well as you would think. I could not get my balance and took a few hard falls and was not even close to learning how to spin. It took time and patience from my instructors, my mother, and on my part. I started out with one lesson a week for over a year and not much ice time.

When I first started taking lessons, my mother took me to the rink every Saturday, and after lessons and some practice time, we went to lunch and then shopping. That's where I got my love for shoes.

I was happy when we bumped it up to two lessons a week and a lot of time on the ice. My grandfather began taking me to the rink because my mother was a single mom and had to work. I would do my best to practice and try not get in the way of the big kids who were faster, stronger and took more lessons than my family could afford. I was happy to skate and was thrilled the days I got to go before or after school.

I did okay as a local competitor. Most of all, I had fun and could not imagine a life without skating. It was part of my routine. During the school year, it was skating then school. In the summer it was skating, then on the boat with my grandfather. The rink was a safe, positive environment to grow up in.

I wanted to start competing, so I needed more practice time. Since my mother was a single mom with a full-time job, my grandfather was designated skating chauffeur. I am still amazed at how much he did so I could skate. I could never repay him for all the time he lost in his personal life. My grandfather, Luke Gallo, was long retired, and I am sure he had much better things to do. Yet he never complained. My grandfather just had one request, and it was not to give up. He taught me this by the way he lived. He was a World War II veteran who received a Purple Heart for being wounded and a Bronze Star for bravery in the fight at Normandy. He asked the soldiers to cover him because there was a badly wounded soldier on the ground, and he was not going to leave him to die on the battlefield. They did cover him, but he was shot. Both he and the soldier he retrieved survived. They were hospitalized and recovered in Germany and went back to battle. He was not the type of person to give up. He was my hero. If it were not for his commitment to my skating, I would not be living the American Dream. In many ways, he saved my life, too.

Learning these life lessons was not always easy. There were plenty of times I had doubts, and I wanted to give up. All my friends were doing other sports. When I had a boyfriend I wanted to spend time with, I did not want to get up early and go to the skating rink. I worked hard, but sometimes it took so long just to land one jump, it was discouraging. I never felt I had natural talent. Still, I tried my best, even when I came in last place. Thanks to my family encouraging me not to give up, I now have my dream job.

I stopped skating for a while in my late teens after I graduated high school. I went back and skated a public session once or twice a week for fun, never thinking I would be a hockey instructor for many years to come.

I was offered a job at the rink where I still work before they even had the ice put down. A woman power skating instructor hired me. I had admired her my whole life and was pleased she wanted me to work for her. I quit my receptionist job at a car dealership, leaving my security and health benefits behind.

I have been teaching at the same rink for over twenty-five years, and I am happier than ever. After twenty-five years at the same company, people usually get a gift, like a gold watch or a crappy pen. I got something much more valuable—memories that will last a lifetime, friends, and the feeling of being part of a special family.

First Lesson

I have done so many jobs in the last twenty-five years other than being a skating instructor, none of which were in shoe sales. I had to take on many part-time jobs, so I could still skate and pay the bills. I was a waitress, preschool teacher, and did a stint in promotional sales. I worked in the offices for an auto body shop and a transmission shop. I was even a wine salesman. I was not very good at any these jobs. Pardon the pun, I was just skating by to earn extra money. My job as a skating instructor was where my passion lay.

I worked for a bank when I first started out. It was my first full-time job. I really did not like it very much, but took the job knowing I would not have to work weekends or holidays. It was okay. I was a filing clerk to start and then worked in the loan department. It was boring and uneventful. I remember scanning in documents and falling asleep at the desk. I hope my old boss does not read this. I guess I should not worry too much. I got laid off with over twenty other people after working there for more than two long years.

I started teaching, thinking it would be a great part-time job. I could make some extra cash while I was looking for work. I knew going back into an office would be like putting me in a cage. I am not very good at sitting still. I am surprised I am sitting here typing for this long without popping up every five minutes like a piece of toast.

Teaching my first lesson, like the first time I slid my feet into a high heel, I was not very good at it. I was awkward and unsure of myself. Walk on heels the first time, I wobbled like a newborn giraffe, trying to walk straight up, with my long neck way in front of my body. It was all wrong, and so was my first lesson.

In the first lesson I gave, I showed my student the wrong way to get up after she fell. I was thankful a more experienced instructor came over and corrected me. She explained how to teach the proper technique to get up after a fall. I could have really hurt a child. It was lesson learned for the both of us. After that, I learned and observed the other instructor's lessons. I was lucky they had known me since I was a kid and they liked me enough to let me follow them around while they taught. It was a great way to get tips on the correct way to teach.

When I first became a skating instructor over twenty-five years ago, I did not think my career would last this long or take so many twist and turns. I started out doing tot group lessons and teaching children how to march on the ice. I was good at playing with the kids but really had no clue how to teach skating. I was animated and sang while we marched across the ice-cold rink. That was all I was really good at. It took a long time on a steep learning curve to become the instructor I am today.

At the rink where I work, we have a preschool. The preschool not only had school classes but came down once a week for skating lessons. I got to work in the classrooms and on the ice for a few years. It was the best thing to happen to me. I learned a bulk of my teaching skills from being around the preschoolers. I learned an understanding of children's feelings, patience and how to get someone who clearly does not want to be on the ice to skate and love it. I even got to design the sets for the ice skating shows they put on for their parents and family members. That was the hardest job I have ever had. It gave me the best hands-on work experience. I worked in the school for four years and continued the on-ice classes for twenty years. In those twenty years, I have done countless classes, picked up over a hundred children, and dried more tears than I could ever count, and I put on forty shows, the last one ending a year after my son's show. I figured that was a good way to end my preschool days. It was fun but very hard on your body.

How I got back into teaching power skating was a stroke of luck. It just so happened the hockey classes needed more instructors. So I grabbed my old hockey skates and started teaching the hockey classes. Before long, I was approached by my students' parents to start teaching private lessons. I was power skating when I first started to teach. After the first five years of teaching, I was doing a lot more figure skating lessons and few power skating lessons.

This was when I started to become a stronger and more knowledgeable instructor, learning to perfect my teaching skills and learning from other instructors how to get better.

Years went by and the more advanced my students got, the more involved my lessons became, having to teach more than just the basics. It was challenging, learning different techniques.

It has been a long time since the first lesson I taught. I have grown so much as an instructor and a person, striving to do my best with every passing day. Thankfully, I still go to work with a positive attitude and a smile on my face, even with the early morning sessions. Coffee helps. I tell my students it is my happy juice, but to be honest, I am happiest being on the ice with them.

No Pain, No Gain

No pain, no gain. That saying holds true with heels and hockey skates. Skaters, in general, are a tough breed and so are the women who wear high heels all night long and after a night of hard-core dancing can still walk out of the venue without a limp.

I have seen guys get stitched up on the bench then are out playing the next shift. Personally, I have had over twenty stitches and numerous bruises from years of skating. My feet also endured countless wedding receptions in which I danced almost every song without flicking off my shoes and exposing my real height.

Breaking in a new pair of hockey skates and a new pair of heels are much the same. If you have never had the pleasure to break in one or the other, the pain is like putting your foot in a sneaker four sizes too small and running a marathon. For both, it seems to hit the side of the foot and my toes with the most blistering pain upon breaking them in. I can compare it to putting your foot into vice and turning it with every step or stride your foot can endure.

Those heels and hockey skates look so pretty busting out of the gate. Your feet even may feel okay at first. After a few laps around the dance floor in heels or a few laps around the rink, my feet feel like the wrapping paper that has been given to a small child on Christmas morning, badly ripped to shreds and wrinkled up into the smallest ball. Your feet feel as if they are being crushed in a garbage compactor. With every agonizing step or push off, your face shows the agony of defeat.

Breaking in skates is one of my least favorite parts of my job. Not only does it cause unpleasant working conditions, but I feel like a newbie skater reaching to find my balance. Getting new skates is like moving into a new home. You are never quite comfortable until you settle in.

I never got into baking my skates in all the years of skating. When I first started skating, we did not have that option. You just had to power through and break in your skates by skating in them. Baking skates is like putting them in an Easy-Bake oven. When the bell goes off on the little oven, your brand new skates come popping out instead of a cupcake. You wedge your foot into the hot skate, and it molds to your foot. In a hot minute, you got a skate that will hurt a little less than if you wear them cold out of the box. I am not buying it. I see people easy-baking and still skating like they have tacks in their skates. It is the old-fashioned way for me, skate. Although I may buy into baking my heels!

Buying skates is one of my least favorite things to do. Not just for the fact I hate to break them in, but it is costly. I can get a few great shoe bargains and a new outfit for what you can spend on a new pair of skates. I buy new skates about every ten years. I'm glad I do not do that with my heels. I cannot go a month without buying shoes. It is retail therapy for me. Everyone has different ways to reward themselves—a nice meal, a bubble bath, a massage, a beer. Mine is new shoes, never new skates.

I am thankful for my old skates. They may look worn out and ugly, but after a while, it feels like I am wearing my bedroom slippers. My heels never felt that good no matter how long I stuffed my feet in them. I am glad it is that way with my skates instead of my heels. I am in my skates a lot more. On the weekends, I am on the ice for six hours per day. I prefer not being a moody, cranky troll because I am cringing with every agonizing push on my skates.

The foot pain is not the only pitfall with instructing or being a fashion diva. As instructors and women who enjoy the latest fashion trends, we put our bodies through all sorts of abuse. Back pain is a common problem for heel enthusiasts and instructors alike.

Walking on heels pushes you onto the balls of your foot, creating an uncomfortable back pain after long periods of time. Older women I have spoken to have confessed it was the heels they wore in their younger days that caused their back pain. Chiropractors must love fashionistas and skaters.

My back has been twisted like a pretzel trying to save numerous kids and adults from slipping and falling to the hard ice. It is a normal reaction to want to save anyone from descending at a rapid speed onto a hard surface. It happens so quickly that you are never in the correct position—knees bent, arms stretched and at the ready like a second basemen waiting for the batter to smoke a pitcher. It is always awkward, and you look like you are trying to snatch a pizza from falling off a counter onto a dirty floor. Your body flops like a fish out of water, and your arms fly around like they are on fire.

I hate to admit, as I get older, I wake up with these odd new aches. If my knees and hips could talk, they would scream, "Lay off! You are not as young as you used to be and if you do not take care of us, we will have you rolling in a wheelchair in fifteen more years!" Everyone needs breaks, but things get complicated in the winter months and when students are getting ready for tryouts. You need to work to pay the bills but also need to relax so you can keep skating for years to come. It is a balancing act that is not always the easiest. You want to show you are strong and not show the pain is getting to you. Being in such a tough sport, I never wanted to give the perception of being weak. It is hard to use the excuse I cannot make it to work today because my tootsies hurt.

Is it worth the pain? For me, yes. I love my job and hope I can do it until I am ninety. I may not be as fast as I am now, but I hope I can enrich students' lives for a long time to come. As far as my heels go, I hope I can wear them as long as I can walk. I love to light up a room, not just with my smile, but with an awesome pair of heels. Hair flowing, my dress fitting my body style and the occasion, I finish off my look with a great pair of heels. It is like the bow on a beautifully wrapped gift.

APPEARANCE

You may not have a million dollars, but you can look like you do, dressing in designer clothes and driving an expensive sports car. You may only be able to ski on a bunny slope, but you can buy the newest gear and look like a pro sitting by a warm fire in the chalet.

I am not a millionaire, but I like to carry myself as one. I like to dress nice and neat and be in style. My grandmother always told me, if your shoes were "up to date" you will always be in style. You can pair a trendy heel with a plain outfit and look like you just walked off the runway.

This holds true when you go to work. Some of us wear uniforms, suits, or street clothes. As a hockey instructor, I am required to wear my rink's logo. So ninety percent of the time, I am working in oversized sweat pants, layers under my warm winter jacket, and my broken-in hockey skates. It is appropriate attire for the work I do. I try not to look feminine. Being in a male-dominated sport, I want my work to stand out, not my appearance.

I am not sure of what the perception of me really is. Looking the part on the ice is not hard. It is off the ice when I am in my street clothes or dressed up for a night on the town, I do not look like a hockey instructor. It is funny. I will change after being on the ice, and some of my students do not recognize me in my clothes and heels. It is like having two different identities—hockey coach and some lady that is off to the mall.

Most kids could care less what you look like or what you are wearing as long as you are good to them. They look up to you as a coach. That is why is it so important to care about them and what you are doing. Over the years, I have gotten comments on poor wardrobe choices, ugly hats I have worn, and even my funky glasses. These days I try to be plain so we can chat about skating instead of fashion. I leave that for when I am off the ice.

For a figure skater or hockey instructor, the main stream of customers is children. Dealing with them can be challenging at times. You always have to have a calm demeanor. Children really pick up on your energy.

Skating coaches are not like school teachers who have a child for a school year or semester. We have them for years. The longest I have had a student was fourteen years. That is a long time, and you develop strong bonds. I was teaching another student for over seven years, and after we stopped lessons together, we kept in touch as I do with most of my students. We were having lunch out somewhere when she told me, "I did not wear a lot of make-up, because you did not, and I never tried smoking because you never smoked." From that moment on, I realized how I conducted myself really affects my students. Until then, the thought never crossed my mind. Since that conversation, I realized the importance of looking and acting in a way that is positive to my students. I never thought of myself as a role model, but we all are for our younger generation.

As coaches, we should always act as if we are being videotaped. With cell phones as popular as they are, I am sure I have been in more videos than I can imagine while teaching my lessons. Parents video their children for monumental reasons. I hope my hair looked good.

Sometimes no matter what we do, we just cannot always look professional. Let's face it, falls can be funny. We shriek at first when someone slips and falls, then we laugh. Think about all those funny homemade videos on YouTube. Being around an ice rink, you are bound to see some very funny falls, especially when it is one of us instructors.

I remember one parent taping his son's lesson that I was teaching. I was trying to bend over to draw a line on the ice and lost my balance. Not only did I fall on my rear end, but I did one of those falls where you bounce a little then fall on your butt and bounce twice. It was not a graceful fall. It was funny. That night when I got home from work, they sent me the footage of my mishap that I did not even know was caught on video. Looking back at it, I'm glad no obscenities came flying out of my mouth.

I had only been teaching for about a year when an older boy came up to the office for power skating lessons. I introduced myself and accompanied him to the ice for our first lesson together. I was talking a good game about edges and how I can teach him how to hockey stop. I had on my hockey jacket that had INSTRUCTOR in bold letters on the back, my hockey skates with the blade guards on. Not realizing I had not taken the blade guards off my skates, I took a doozy of a first step on the ice and on my ass. I looked up with humility and told him he could go back up to the front desk and request another instructor. We laughed and had a lot more lessons together, and he keeps in touch. I even taught his son in group lessons.

It is hard not to wear your problems on your sleeve. We all have problems, and I know sometimes it is challenging to pretend things are peachy when you feel your world is collapsing around you. I try to go to work with the attitude, the problems I have today will not be the same problems I have a month from now. Like in any job, it is not always easy to check your emotions at the door. It is hard to smile and pretend you do not want to go back to bed and pull the covers over your head and sleep until all your problems magically disappear. Life at the rink, or in general, does not work that way. When you are preaching be positive, you have to act like it, even when you do not feel your best.

In all of my years of doing the job I love so much, I have been through some hard times personally. I had been through two divorces, stressful breakups, financial distress but the worst time came with the loss of both of my grandparents. They were more like my parents. They raised me, and I was with them for the first twenty-six years of my life. I was devastated when they passed away only weeks apart. Getting over all of the bad times, the one stable thing I could depend on was my job. I had been at the same rink for so long, it was like home, the place I felt most secure. No matter what was going on in my life, I could go to the rink and escape from it all and focus on the work.

These are the things you do not see on the surface. The outfits we wear, pretty figure skating dresses, hockey gear, or coach's jackets are only shells. That is why everything is not always how it appears. Even the heavy doors of the rink are not an entrance to a cold tundra. Instead, it is the place I see the most warmth. Parents and grandparents watch from behind the thick glass or in the stands, while their children learn skills that will last a lifetime, like how to work hard to achieve your goals, how to be part of a team, and how to lose with dignity.

A Man's World

It is funny how working in a male-dominated world you try to dull your look. Okay, I am not strutting on the ice in five-inch stilettos, but I try not to wear too much make-up or form fitting clothes. I try to blend in. But it is hard not to stand out, being the only five-foot eight-inch woman with blond hair and hockey skates.

Being a figure skater first, I worked with more women on the ice than men. If you have ever worked with women and men, you can see the differences. I am lucky to have worked with both women and men. I would not say one gender is better to work with than another; they are just very different. Women are more sensitive like me, where men are rough around the edges but in a great way. With the guys, you always know what they think about you because they have no problem telling you exactly what is on their minds. I kind of like that about them. You do not have to guess what they want to say. They just blurt it out.

I have had the pleasure to work with some amazing women. They were not only talented and accomplished skaters, but they also shared their gifts with others. Working alongside my female coworkers helped me develop into a strong coach. I have worked with two women in particular who really shaped the way I teach. Pegeen Creede was a national competitor in her own right. She has mentored me in figure skating. I could not have had a better teacher. She has an eye for watching a jump and being able to make a correction in a split second. Working with Michelle Schmitz-Armando has been extremely beneficial. Her mind works fiercely not only on the task at hand but the best and fastest way to get to the goal. I copy and modify her figure skating drills to help my hockey players become the best they can be. It was not just for their extensive knowledge of the sport, but the way to make a novice skater into a fierce competitor.

You can say it is a woman's touch. Learning how to bring out the best in each individual skates is a valuable asset to becoming a great instructor. Most of the women I have worked with taught me that skill. That is a very difficult skill. I like to say every lesson I change my hat. I work at being able

22

to determine what works best for each student, whether it's a soft tune, an authority figure. Does a student need to learn verbally by explaining drill, or visual by showing the skater what to do physically? Woman are tuned in with emotions. That makes them wonderful in at this job.

I started doing hockey/power skating lessons when I first became an instructor. I did not love the work I was putting out like I do now. I needed to mature as a person and coach. I looked at it as a fun job. I needed to understand the basic principles and grow.

That was one of the things I love the most about power skating. It is so much more involved than you may think. In the beginning, I never thought about doing so much edge work until I was watching the figure skating coaches. They were training their skater's speed. That is the key to developing hockey players. You need to do those drills the figure skaters were doing so accurately to learn how to get the balance and speed. As the years went on, I got more meticulous with my teaching style. It was like a new challenge for me to make up drills that hockey players can utilize in game situations to make them more effective players.

I tell all my new students, I do some different drills, but I swear I will make you a better skater. Some stick with it, and others think it is crazy and they do not want to spend the extra time doing the edge-work drills.

I have a student doing a drill using both feet with one not moving and the other pushing on the inside and outside edges. The drill looks weird. So one of my students turned to me and asked if I was making him do a wacky figure skating move. I had to laugh, and I said to him, "Honestly, I was a figure skater for thirty years and not once did I do that move on my figure skates. But figure skaters use similar drills to get the same results."

I can recall being at the rink doing a lesson with a ten-year-old student, and at the doorway of the ice rink stood his father intently watching the lesson. Every correction I made, the father barked over me to instruct his son. It was disrespectful. I felt he was trying to overpower me because I was a woman. I do not think he would have been as vocal if a male was teaching his son. It was quite embarrassing. It was making the other parents in the rink uncomfortable. Not knowing what else to do, I skated over to the father, took off my jacket with the rink logo on it and handed it to him. I was polite, but told him, "Would you like to do my job? I got this. I am really good at it." He just laughed and let me do my lesson while he looked on in silence. We did not have too many lessons after that, but it did form a mutual respect.

The guys I work with have a different teaching style from what I do. I focus more on edge-work and balance, and the speed at the end of my lessons. It depends on what a skater develops and responds better with. The guys have a more intimidating presence, where I am lighter, and I try not to yell unless it is in a large group lesson. Even then, it is only so all the students can hear my instruction.

When I first started doing more power skating lessons, the guys took notice. I wore my hockey skates and hardly put on my figure skates. I was working closer to the area designated for hockey players. I am not sure, but I think I became a threat like a little wave in the ocean. I know that because one of the guys asked if I was not getting along with the figure skating department and why was I doing more power skating? I said things were fine. I was just trying to change things up. Some were more welcoming than others at first, and I tried my hardest to break down the walls.

These days when I go to work, the guys are amazing to work with. I get high fives when I skate by, and even better, I get a lot of hugs when I get on the ice to teach them. The guys feel confident enough to confide in me with their personal lives. I am happy to listen and not give silly emotional advice. I am not there to be a know-it-all and say what I do is better. It is different. I also have the pleasure to work with several of their students. Working together can only help a student grow. I glad to work for the greater good.

My changing things up turned out to change things a lot. I am at what I think may be the tail end of my figure skating career. I did not plan it that way. It sort of flipped almost overnight. I started to do the hockey classes, and I got more private lessons from them. I was wearing my hockey skates more than my figure skates as each week went by. I was enjoying my job more than ever. It was like a new toy. It was a fresh start, like I was not doing the same job for twenty-five years. I was excited and truly enjoying myself. I found a new start to my long career, which I thought was at a dead end. That's why I was trying so many other jobs, but now I found this new love, and I appreciate it more.

I am now with the guys all the time, and I love them more than ever. The guys have been so great, and they do not even seem to mind all the drills I do. I think students benefit from having someone teach the hockey skills with speed, edges, and where to direct your balance. Who knows? Maybe the guys think my balancing drills are good because I wear high heels, and I had to learn a thing or two walking in those things.

OVERCOMING OBSTACLES

Did you ever see a little girl trying on her mom's high heels for the first time? It is cute watching her wobble with her arms out trying to catch her balance with every step. Eventually, she starts to get the hang of it. She drags the oversized shoes with her tiny foot pressed up to the toe along the floor and acts like she owns it.

We all have obstacles in every journey we take, whether it is being a parent, finding the love of our lives, finding satisfaction in our jobs, or even finding ourselves.

I consider myself pretty blessed now to be a hockey instructor. It was not always what I wanted. The struggles I went through to get here were not always so easy.

Hockey is a male-dominated sport. Growing up, very few girls played hockey. I did not know any. I just knew of a select group of women who taught both power skating and figure skating. The main pioneer who inspired these women to teach power skating was the first NHL female hockey coach, Barbara Williams. As a child I idolized Barbara.

At the rink where I practiced when I was growing up, they had a news article hanging in the office. I used to stare at it. It had a black and white photo of four women, with Barbara in the middle. As a young girl, I was in awe. I wanted to be like all of them someday.

They all paved the way for women power skating instructors. It became more acceptable for a woman to teach hockey players. It was like a transition. The figure skaters were onto something. They can teach a hockey player balance, speed, and how to get on edges.

It was years later when I ended up proudly working for Barbra Williams at the rink where I still work. She told me that to teach hockey you have to wear hockey skates. This was a challenge. I had very little time before my job started to learn to be proficient on a different kind of blade. That is like telling a painter he can only use crayons on his canvas. I was a mess. I felt like that little girl walking in her mom's heels.

I practiced a lot and fell a lot. With determination driving me, I got better. In fact, I got good enough to start standing in on the woman's power skating lessons that I admired as a young girl. They were so fast and made corrections to enhance a hockey player's skills. They covered things I would have never taught them to do.

I started out doing hockey group lessons. I used to get insulted when parents would ask for a guy and not a girl instructor. Now it is funny to me. With all the strides women have made, we still cannot get over that stereotype. I no longer take it to heart. I just say, "Let my work speak for itself." I am confident my teaching is as good as, if not better than, a man's.

The biggest obstacle I had to overcome in my life is that I am blind in one eye. The muscle that connects my right to the brain did not develop from birth, leaving me blind in that eye. That causes my depth perception to be off. Looking out in the distance or close up, someone with two eyes can tell how far away the object would be from them. Also being blind in one eye causes difficulties with balance so even everyday walking can be troubling. I consider myself fortunate I was able to compensate because I have to overcome this. I adjusted at a young age. I was not clumsy, it just took me a little longer to walk than the average toddler. Skating, however, was a challenge. I had to work harder to accomplish goals.

As I mentioned before, you just adjust. That is what I did. I adjusted. I remember an eye doctor telling my mother I would never skate. I am so glad she did not listen. I was not allowed to do contact sports growing up. I did them anyway. I cannot hit a ball with pinpoint accuracy, but I can hold my own. I played beach volleyball for a recreational team. I held my own and had a good time doing it. I am happy I never missed out on that experience to be a skater.

My students and adults notice can notice my one eye floats off a little. It happens mainly when I am tired. Kids are so honest and will ask me about it. Some adults will ignore it, trying not to be rude or move into what they think is my line of vision. I have no problem informing anyone of my blind eye. I am not ashamed anymore about the way my eyes look.

HEELS & HOCKEY SKATES Woman POWER Skater

I used to be embarrassed and felt like everyone was looking at me. I like to tell my students the story of the eye doctor who did not think I could skate. I tell them all the time, "Do not let anyone tell you that you cannot do something. If you want to do it, you can." So I did. I am a hockey instructor.

Once when the rink first opened for business, a man asked for me by saying, "Is Kim I available?" The woman he asked was so offended thinking that he called me "Kim eye" not knowing he wasn't referring to my blind eye. He called me Kim I referring to my first initial of my very long last name. At that time I worked with two other women named Kim. It was funny.

So it really does not matter what gets in our way, as long as it does not hold us back from what we want in life. All of us have obstacles. It is the way we deal with them that makes the difference. As for me, I know without these obstacles I would not be the instructor I am today.

HOCKEY SMELL

Sitting in a new car, you just want to take a deep breath and soak in the "new car smell." Everyone has a scent that results in a good feeling—new baby smell, puppy breath, coffee in the morning, or a fragrant spring flower. For me, it is opening a box of new leather heels. I just want to indulge the "new shoe smell." The smell may be different for each individual, but the actions are the same. You take in that long sniff, and you can hear your breath engulf the fragrance. Your chest puffs out, and the softness of the aroma fades slowly, leaving behind a happy memory and a big smile.

Then there are not-so-good smells, like garbage dumps, low tide, two-day-old used sweat sock, and the dreaded "hockey smell." I think that is what evil smells like. If you have never smelled it, it gives off an odor like vinegar, old sneaker, and rotten egg all rolled together, and potent enough to cause straight hair to instantly curl. On a normal day, you can walk into an ice rink, and the crisp air is refreshing, almost welcoming. That's when no hockey games are taking place. When the guys are playing, the hockey smell can be so pungent in that same rink it can make your eyes water. The rink is big enough you would not think the smell of the guys would float up into the air, but it just stays there, hunting your nose leaving you gasping as you walk by.

As long as I can remember, I could not stand that smell. When I was young and had to skate after a hockey game took place, I would be so annoyed to have to breathe in the gross hockey smell. I can still remember doing my first few laps around the rink with my glove covering my nose like an oxygen mask. Pressing the glove so hard to my face, I must have looked as if I was going to swallow the mitten and cough out a hair ball. As the guys walked out of the rink with their hockey bags slung over their shoulders, my face said it all—wash your equipment and hose yourselves off. It was one of the main reasons I never wanted to play a pickup game with friends. I would have to borrow someone's hockey gear because I am not going out and buying the expensive equipment needed for as little as I would use it. The very thought of putting on any of the pads with that smell attached to it was enough to keep me from joining in the fun. It is kind of ironic how I work in a field where I am undoubtedly going to be with hockey smell.

Do not get me wrong. We instructors do not always smell like we just jumped out of an Irish Spring shower. The ladies and I have a little pro room to put our skates on. It is a small, duck-your-head-or-you-will-smack-it-on-a-very-hard-metal-beam women's locker room under the steps of the rink. It is kind of like it was built for tall hobbits. I admire my co-workers for their amazing talents but not their feet smell. Most of us do not wear socks in our skates. I wear the ever so sexy, knee-high stockings. The minute you take your foot out of the skate, it releases a foot smell that can give a hockey player a run for the money. It comes up and smacks you right in the face. When we all are getting ready to go out and work on the ice, we can really smell up the little joint containing the odor in one tiny steel room. I am very thankful for Febreeze and Odor-Eaters.

Being a professional skater does have its downfalls. Our occupational hazards are: falling in front of students and trying to pretend it does not hurt; getting hit by a puck while looking like it is a normal occurrence; getting punched in the kisser by a skater who is flinging her arms to keep her balance; and helping students put on their equipment and skates. Throughout the years, I have smelled some foul odors. The big trick is to appear as if they do not stink and have your face not crinkle as you're trying to speak to the parents about proper equipment. These odors do not just come from the big hockey players but from little kids too. I am always amazed how such a big stink can come out of such a small child.

I think we all can attest I really hate hockey smell. No one knows this better than one of my coworkers. We teach power skating in an area in the back of the rink. It is intended for students and instructors. Maybe I mention far too often how stinky the players get and how I cannot stand teaching next to them. After all, they are working hard and sweating, and that is what you want them to do.

I was working in the back with a colleague that I admire. He was teaching a teenager who raised hockey smell to an art. This kid had a gift for clearing a room, he smelled so bad. My coworker thought it would be funny to have him do all his drills next to my student and me. Since my student was not moving as well, I was stuck in one spot. If I would go left, my colleague had his kid practice hockey stops to the left. If I went right, he would do right side drills. He could hardly stand up on his skates he was laughing so much watching me wiggle as I was trying to hold my breath. The more I would try to get away, the more he would send his student to get close to me without him knowing. He was enjoying watching me trying to keep my composure. Now writing this, I've reminded myself to get back at him.

Hockey smell is not pleasant, but it is a fact of life. With anything else, you have to take the good with the bad. If we think about it, the bad never outweighs the good. Perception is key. Try to find the good no matter what situation you're in, and the bad is never as bad as you think.

Hockey Mom

I'm not sure if I fit the mold of a typical hockey mom. I wear high-heeled boots to the rink instead of what I should wear—warm and comfy boots. I like sitting in the freezing stands with a hot beverage, layers of clothes, and my fuzzy blanket, clapping my monstrous, furry mittens together while cheering on my son.

I do not get to see as many of my son's games as I would like to. It is not that I do not want to go, but game times seem to conflict with my work schedule being a skating instructor. I do bring my son to the rink with me most of the time. He goes one way, and I am off in the other direction. The rink is a familiar, safe, and comfortable environment for both my son and me.

Even before Luke was born, he was ice skating. Not that he knew it. He must have thought the waters were rocky in the womb the times I was skating around while pregnant. I imagine it was kind of like a mini wave pool.

At first, I did not show any signs of being pregnant, and I did not want my clients to know. I was afraid they might leave me for another instructor. That happens more than you think. I saw it with other female instructors. Clients believe you cannot give their child the attention they need, or that you are going to abandon ship and not come back to teaching after you have the baby. I kept the pregnancy a secret for the first months.

It is sad that women should feel that way in any business. Being in a male-dominated occupation, I wanted to hide it even more, and not show any sign of weakness. Appearance is everything. It is not always easy to keep that hard-core image when you are trying to grow a baby inside of you and glow.

Since I wear a bulky jacket and oversized sweat pants when I teach, no one could tell I was hiding the extra weight. I was getting large rapidly. I could not help it. I was eating like I was feeding a hockey team in my belly.

One of my coworkers was walking past me, and in his extremely heavy accent, he said to me, "Why are you getting so fat?" After being a tad bit insulted, I laughed and told him I was pregnant.

After that, I let everyone in on the news. For me, it was better to let people think I was pregnant than thinking I was stress eating because my husband at the time was being shipped off to Iraq.

I was getting so big that skating was getting harder with every passing day. I had to wear a coworker's husband's extra-large jacket because I could not fit into anything that had the rink emblem on it. I was in a meeting, and we were all told it is mandatory for all instructors to always wear something on with the rink logo if we are instructing. Then my boss looked over at me and said, "With the exception of Kim right now, due to the fact that she cannot fit into anything we have." I could have fit into a hockey jersey now I that I think about it.

After a while, figure skates were not an option. My figure skates were way too tight. I had to wear my hockey skates. Hockey skates are wider and much more comfortable. I was not being too picky. I wanted to be on the ice with the kids.

Putting my skates on was challenging with my huge belly in the way. I could not bend over to get the skates on my feet. I would try to put my leg all the way to one side and hook my foot onto my skate. It looked as if I was lassoing my skate to my foot, as if my foot was first prize in a calf roping contest. I could not reach straight down to lace up, so I tried the side tie, kicking my foot to the side of me on the bench and lacing up. This work for a few weeks with the bow to the side of my skate. Eventually, I got so big I was unable to put on my skates. I would pay one of the kids a dollar to put them on and take them off. If you ask me now, I think I should have paid them more.

The day gave birth to Luke, I was expecting to go to the rink that day to say hello. At that point, I could not skate anymore. My balance was way off, and the doctors did not want me to put the baby at risk. Being lonely, I went to spend time at the rink in my comfort zone. Later that day, I was told I had to go the hospital, and I had an emergency C-section. The first thing I did was call the rink. I spoke to the receptionist whom I had known for a long time. "I think I am going to have the baby today," I said. They got the news before my husband did. That was the first place I called. They are family to my son and me.

Three weeks later I was back on the ice. My son was in his stroller being babysat by one of the moms who happened to be in the cafe area of the rink that day.

I am used to the odd hours and so is my son. He was born into the skating world. Skaters train in the early mornings. You go whenever you can get ice time.

I take my son with me to the ice rink a few early mornings each week, so I can work and he can practice. He is great about getting up in the morning most of the times. I feel guilty, waking him up at the crack of dawn so I'm not late for work. Once we get there, he has a great time, and it is hard to get him off the ice or take him away from his friends.

Weekends are a must in my line of work, and after school during the week. It does make it hard to go to parties and after school events. I just say it is the nature of the beast. On the light side, I do get out of some events I'd rather not attend with the excuse, "Sorry have to go to work." I really do not mind the hours. I've gotten used to it. When I tell someone I have to be at work at six thirty on the ice, they cringe. As long as I got to bed early and I am armed with a cup of coffee, it is not so bad.

Being a hockey mom is one of my favorite jobs, even if I do not get to all the games and I screw up the times a lot. I am thankful I get so much help from the rink and staff when I mess up. They are so understanding and supportive of me. I am a single mom with a great support system—my son's dad, my family, and the family we have at the rink. I am amazed how much everyone pitches in with things as simple as tying skates or just watching over my son. It does take a village to raise a child. Luckily for Luke and me, we are in the great village, the rink.

MONEY, MONEY, MONEY

My heels can be expensive, but not as expensive as my skates. My figure skates at a coach's discount with the blades were over eight hundred dollars, so I thought I got a bargain on my hockey skates at only two hundred dollars.

Because I have been skating since I was ten years old, I have had many skating lessons. For me, lessons have paid off. I turned it into my career. If your child does not get to skate professionally, what they take away from is more important—a sense of accomplishment, and responsibility. Those lessons are priceless. I know for me, it kept me out of a lot of trouble and taught me to be responsible. I never smoked or did drugs, so my performance on the ice was not compromised.

Lessons are also a big expense. I know firsthand. I have an eight-year-old who just started travel hockey, and has been taking lessons from another coach.

In a perfect world, I would be able to teach my son power skating, but we do not work well together. We have a great relationship, and I would like to keep it that way.

It is not that we did not try. We had a few lessons together. Every lesson went the same way—all he wanted to do was race me, and every time I did a drill with him, he would skate away. It was frustrating for both of us. The lessons were no more than fifteen minutes and ended with me yelling and him crying. I was more upset with myself for being hard on him. I was not like that with my students. I could not understand why I was so hard on him. I have more patience with my students than I did my own son. I felt awful and upset that he did not want to take my advice. Needless to say, my son has another power skating instructor, and I am happy to pony up the dough.

The big expenses come once a year during the slow lesson month of June. My skating insurance, annual club fees, membership and testing for the Professional Skating Association. To work at my rink, they hold us to high standards and require us to take a test online every year. At first, I hated this idea, but now I kind of like it. I feel like I am worth more to my students if I am better educated. I hate paying for them, but it is well worth it. I have been learning new ways to teach, and the information I get about how to treat injuries can only help me improve my lessons.

I have to admit this year taking the group lesson test, I was cocky. At this point, I have taught over a thousand group lessons. The test should have been a walk in the park or an easy skate around the rink. I went to take the test and only halfway read it. I was on my phone playing games and texting. I failed it not once, but twice until I realized I better read the information and start paying attention. It made me think. I still have a lot to learn even as long as I have been doing my job. There is always room for improvement.

Some people spend a lot of money on a college education. I did go to college and almost have my associate's degree in graphic design. To be honest, I do not have a clue about that field. I really liked the drawing classes I got to take. I went to community college first, then transferred to a private school near my home. The school recently closed. So I guess the education I got on the ice and all the money my grandparents and parents paid for was well worth it. I am using all that training to my benefit now.

All the skating lessons and early morning practices did keep me out of trouble. I was not able to hang out with friends until all hours of the night. I knew I had to skate in the morning. I did not ever smoke because I was worried I would be winded on the ice. I had a hard enough time getting through a two-minute program. The last thing I wanted was to hang over the side of the boards gasping for air. I was bad enough I looked like I needed an oxygen tank after a hard skate. I was breathing heavier than a St. Bernard on a hot summer day. The last thing I needed was to smoke and make that feeling any worse. So the investment was worth it. I am very healthy and live a healthy lifestyle. That is priceless.

I do save money on a gym membership. It is like I multitask. I work and work out at the same time. Chasing after the hockey players, you get great exercise. At times I feel like I just did an hour of a nonstop aerobics class and all I did was a few laps at full speed around the rink. Heading into summer, I seem to skate harder with my students. I joke and tell them I need to lose a few pounds for the beach. This is not that far off. It beats running on a treadmill for me.

I am fortunate now. I built up a good business and can pay the bills and even have a little left over for shoe shopping. As long as I do not over spend, I will do okay. I never did my job with the intent I would make millions. I did it for the love of the sport and kids. For what it is worth, I hit the job jackpot.

WOMEN IN POWER

For young girls, it is great to look up to a positive role model. As a ten-year-old girl, I did not look up to supermodels or actresses in the most beautiful heels and gorgeous outfits. I looked up to a small group of women who skated at my rink. These select woman had a powerful impact on my life.

I can remember going to the rink office and looking up at a newspaper article that featured five women in front of a hockey net posing with their hockey skates on. I was amazed. How awesome it was to see a woman in hockey skates. I cannot remember what was written about those ladies, but the photo is still vivid in my memory.

As a student, I would look over and see these women training hockey players. I watched them teach, sometimes losing my concentration on my practice time. Two of the ladies in the photo were my figure skating instructors. As time went on, I got to know all of the women personally.

The woman in the middle of the photo and the woman who forged the pathway for women power skating instructors was Barbara Williams. She was the first NHL hockey skating coach. She was always pleasant to my grandfather and me

As years went by, I was still plugging along as a figure skater, and working a full-time job I dreaded going to every day. Barbara approached me to come and work for her at a new rink that was opening up.

I would have dropped my job if she asked me to sweep the floors at her house. I was elated and could not wait for my new job to start. In the meantime, Barbara told me to learn how to teach hockey. It would make me more of an asset.

I bought my first pair of hockey skates, and I still have them tucked in a closet. The first day on my hockey skates, I must have looked like I did my first time on my mother's high heels. I was wobbly. My push was wrong, and I was not used to a smaller blade. I must have fallen at least a dozen times. To my credit, I kept trying.

I was determined to not let Barbra down and work at the new rink. I so worked hard at getting used to my new way of skating. I watched other power skating instructors for a while. I got much better at power skating with hockey skates. Watching all those lessons, chasing kids, and trying to keep up with the corrections each of the other instructors was making on the student, I had to skate well, or I would miss it.

I was so thrilled working for the new rink. Barbara was the director of the skating school. I was doing a lot of tot and beginner lessons. I was off to a good start.

Shortly after, Barbara left the rink. I remember I was so upset when she left. I was not sure if I was going to keep my job. I was happy there and did not want to leave. I kept my job long after my mentor moved on. I have worked there through six different skating directors and their extremely different views on how to conduct the business. I am still at that same rink, and I am one of five original employees who have been there since the rink opened. I remained at my job even after we changed owners.

I think what made me stay was how much I loved the work I was do-ing. I did not always love all the changes. It was hard to adjust to different people and management styles. I was fortunate. I was well-liked and able to get along with most everyone.

I also owe a debt of gratitude to Suzie Belliveau Hewitt. Growing up, she was my figure skating coach along with Mabs Joseph. Both women were instrumental in my training years.

Suzie was the reason for all the amazing edges I mastered over the years. She is also a power skating coach, and I greatly admired her. She let me follow her around and gave me a wonderful foundation to be not only a figure skating instructor but a power skating instructor as well.

I am certainly not the only woman who has been influenced by these pioneers in the power skating world. There are many of us in the field.

More and more women who started figure skating have also been teaching power skating.

Women power skaters make a compelling argument about the way you learn to play hockey. Skating is your first line of defense. If you cannot skate, you cannot play ice hockey, plain and simple. Who better to teach you than someone who knows balance and edges—a figure skater!

Figure skaters spend countless hours perfecting their craft. They take skating tests, called moves, in the field. Skaters are judged intensely on edge control, patterns, and mainly speed. Also, the things that are most crucial to a hockey player during a game.

In order to learn how to jump and spin you need to learn the basics of skating and what edge you need to be on. Every jump is performed on a specific edge in order to land the jump properly. Learning to stay over an axis is essential to spin. This translates nicely into teaching hockey. Edges and staying over your axis are the very basics of skating correctly.

A woman's touch is a good thing when it comes to power skating. As far as my lessons go, I can be overly annoying but in a good way with my attention to detail. If you are not in the right position or are on the wrong edge, you will not be able to skate accurately or play up to your ability. I have tremendous amounts of patience and stick with a drill until it is correct. If I cannot get a student to do a drill correctly, I will find another way to execute a move properly.

I have spent countless hours teaching players to stop both on their left and right sides. I am so good at it now, I bet them I can get them to stop in less than 5 seconds, and then I time it on the clock.

I try never to yell or get frustrated. I know students are there to succeed, and I want to be a part of the journey. As a woman, I like to over-explain skating techniques, so my students are always on the same page. Kids and adults alike get embarrassed when they do not understand something. As a woman and a mom, I have a lot of compassion, and I know that is why students find it easier to trust me and feel comfortable communicating their problems in skating to me. You will work harder for someone that you trust.

I am among a handful of strong women who teach power skating, and I could not feel more blessed than I do every time I give a lesson. Over the years, it had gotten easier for women to break out of the stereotype that we cannot teach hockey players because we have never played in a game. More and more people are starting to acknowledge the benefit of having female power skating instructors. We know how to convey our skills with accuracy that would enhance any level hockey player.

Even with all these logical reasons, there are still men and women who believe a woman cannot teach hockey. I have heard it more than you would think in my twenty-five years of skating. I do not let it bother me anymore and just smile thinking how ignorant some people can be.

I am sure no one fell more victim to this prejudice more the Barbara.

Barbara Williams first started out as a figure skater and a speed skater. In the late 70s, she became the skating director of a Long Island Ice Rink and has been a skating director of many local ice rinks. Shortly after she met a professional hockey player who played for the New York Islanders, she began to teaching him edge work and power skating. The Islanders' head coach took notice, and after watching her teach, he asked her to coach the NHL team. That is where her amazing career took off.

She was the first female to coach in the NHL. News crews and cameras were on her the first day teaching the team.

"At that moment history was made, not only for me but also for all women," Barbara said. In January 1977, Barbara changed history, creating a path for women who would go on to teach power skating.

To this day, Barbara still supports female power skating instructors like me, not only with all her accomplishments, but with her knowledge, kind words, and positivity.

STYLING

Everyone has their own style. That's what makes us unique. I can strut in a great sling back where others may prefer a wedge. Just as there are different shoe styles, there are different skating styles too.

Shoe styles change all the time, and so do teaching styles. What I used to teach years ago is outdated. Think about how much equipment has changed so we can better master our craft. In that way, our teaching styles need to evolve also. That's why it is important to keep up with the times. This way, you can be the best for your students.

I learn not only from the online testing but from my coworkers. They may have a drill that is effective for what I want my student to excel at. I am great at what I do because I always thrive to learn and grow. I take a lot of pride in my work and love putting out quality.

Just like a classic shoe, there are the basics of teaching that will never go out of style. The basics of skating are a hockey player's foundation and should be mastered before moving on to more difficult skills.

The basics should always include learning a swizzle, so a skater knows how to push his or her weight from front to back on the inside edge of a blade. It is the way to learn how to push off and learn a stride.

Your basics should always include how to stop, and how to maintain balance, and how to go backward.

On all of my first lessons, my students see me spin a quarter. I show them this to give them an understanding of an axis. When I spin the quarter, I tell them, "See the line the quarter is spinning over? That is the axis line and what keeps the quarter from falling. We all have an axis line. It goes from the top of our heads down the middle

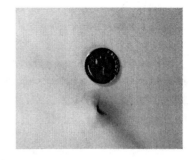

of our bodies." I always tell them to gauge it by keeping one or two feet under your belly button (your axis).

I like to make them walk off the ice because when you walk, your feet are under your belly button. Then I explain that since we are on blades, we have to push out to the sides. In walking, our foot goes in front with one foot under an axis, but in skating, our foot has to push out to the side with one foot under the axis at all times. Balance is the same whether you walk or skate.

It is a simple concept. After a skater comprehends that all of your balance comes from being over your axis, skating becomes easier to understand.

The rink where I work lets us draw on the ice with a washable marker. This is a very helpful tool. I can draw where a body position should be or even a simple line that students can balance their weight over. I also draw circles and squares depending on the drill. If a student can visualize a shape, they can learn a drill more easily. It is helpful for crossovers and turns, too.

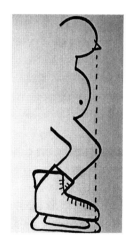

There is a better way to teach edges than when I first started to teach. I used to tell all my students we have two edges, insides and outsides. According to the test I took in the last year, we have eight. This makes more sense to me now, and my skaters have a wonderful understanding of where they need to distribute their weight on the blades. It helps to know all eight edges in order to skate using the whole blade and not just the front or backs of the blade. I tell my students, "Think of your hockey blade like a rocking horse. If you go too far forward, you will fall forward. Too far back, you land on your butt."

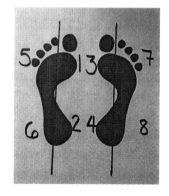

As skaters, we need to utilize the blade not only for balance but also for speed and lateral movement. When students learn the proper position and where to push your weight on the blade, it will benefit them when skating forward and backward, and with lateral moves, crossovers, and turns. Knowledge is power, and the more you know about where to place your weight on the blade, the better you are going perform in a game situation.

As a power skating instructor, you want your skaters to be able to play a game and skate without being distracted or having to concentrate on skating. Players need to focus on the game and what is going on around them, not wondering how am I going to stand up on these skates? Skating, when done properly becomes easy, like walking or running. The more you work on edges, the more skating becomes second nature.

Everyone learns at a different pace, whether it is school work, loving and relationships, or a sport. That is why it is so important for me to know my students and the way they learn. With some students, I can talk them through a drill. Others need to see exactly what needs to be done. Some students need a gentle push where others need a little more understanding.

I cannot stress this enough—repetition is key. The more you are on the ice, the better skater you will become. It is an easy concept. I explain this all the time. I try to encourage my students to practice after their lessons. Muscles have memories, and you can give them good memories from what they learned in the lessons, or keep doing the same thing incorrectly and give your muscles bad memories. Practicing correctly makes perfect.

If you peel an onion, there are a lot of layers. One by one, you eventually expose the onion and get to see what is inside. I believe people are the same. Most of us are a lot deeper on the inside. You will be more willing to learn from special people in your in life whom you trust.

That's what makes this job so interesting. In every lesson, I change my thought process and try to bring out the best in my skater. What works well for one student may not work at all for another.

Maybe there is a life lesson in there too—learn to bring out the best in the people around you. Lift people. Do not try to beat anyone down. You will get much better results.

TESTIMONIALS

Like the different shoes I have in my closet, so are the different students I have come to love over the years.

At this point, I only teach figure skaters. I have had one since she was three years old and she is now graduating high school. Of my other figure skaters, I have taught one for over seven years, and my other is a graduating senior I have instructed for over four years. I could never give up on the girls. The bonds I have created with them are very strong. I am still friendly with the figure skaters I have taught in the past. When the girls come home from college, I am thrilled they want to go to lunch with me. I love hearing how they are flourishing in their adult lives. I was even in several wedding parties. I seem to take on a mommy/friend role in their lives, and I am thrilled about it.

I really do like to get to know my hockey players on a personal level. I enjoy going to their games when I can, or watching videos of the goal they scored. From all the years I have been teaching I always found when I took a personal interest in my students, I could instruct them better and draw out the best in them. Sometimes I feel like I had to change my hat every lesson I do. Some need a push, visuals, or just a hug on a bad day.

I have built many friendships and bonds over the years and am thankful for the experiences with my students.

Paul Blase, professional hockey player (SPHL, Europe), former and current student:
One of the biggest advantages that a hockey player can have is that of being an elite skater. Before I even dressed in hockey gear for the first time, I had the opportunity to learn how to skate with Kim Interdonato through our local rink's basic and advanced skating program. The advantage was immediately apparent when I enrolled in a local house league as one of the best skating players despite having not played. This allowed me to focus on developing my other skills, such as shooting, stick handling, and passing. As a professional hockey player, I have to think that mastering arguably the

most important aspect of our game first has made the success I have seen thus far possible.

I also have to mention the abundance of female power skating instructors not only in my personal experience but among my peers as well. Figure skating is dominated by females. They focused largely on their personal skating abilities as it is key to success in their sport.

Although there are hockey players that are great power skating coaches, why not trust someone who has dedicated their lives solely to the dynamics of skating?

Jenine Venth, mother of Evan, high school hockey player

Hockey is one of the toughest sports to play. There are so many components to playing hockey. The most important is being able to "hockey skate" which is much different from everyday ice skating. My son, Evan, has been skating with Kim for three years now, and their relationship has gone above and beyond skating coach and student. Kim and Evan share the same passion for hockey skating besides the love of the game itself. They work so well together that on lesson days kids and coaches at the rink look for Evan and Kim. Kids ask if they can challenge Evan. Coaches talk to Kim and Even about the results they have every week. Evan made our freshman high school hockey team because of Kim and her skills. Evan and Kim are a special combination with great results. Further evidence of how special Evan and Kim's relationship is that when possible Kim attends Evan's games. Kim's dedication and commitment to all her students go beyond coaching. Kim will always be a part of our "hockey family."

Greg Kozlowski, father of Nick, high school hockey player

My son, Nick, started skating with Kim when he was nearly nine years old. As parents new to hockey and skating in general, we were nervous that he would be greatly behind kids who had tied on skates as soon as they began to walk.

We asked around for recommendations on the best course of acting to get Nick started. "Lessons, lots of lessons," was the common answer from all who provided feedback. But where to go? "Kim, you must go to Kim," was the follow-up response. And so to Kim we went!

The first time on the ice was, of course, nerve-wracking for our son.

The first couple of sessions were more "ice marching" and less "ice skating." What struck us immediately with Kim was her sense of compassion toward a new student, and the encouragement she provided along the way. Milestones were reached, of course—skating forward and backward, crossovers, and what we thought to be impossible, stopping on the weak foot.

More than two years and countless lessons later, Kim has provided Nick with a logical progression in power skating to the point where he is now always one of the most proficient skaters on any team he plays on. Power skating with a strong attention to edge work cannot be picked up during the course of a game. A developing skater needs the guidance from an outside coach. In our case, that's Kim, who strives to continue to build the skill set of the skater as their body matures and the game speeds up. We cannot thank Kim enough for proving Nick with the confidence and support needed to grow as a hockey player. Without her dedication and focus our son wouldn't be nearly the skater that he is today.

Mark Chamberlin, father of Cole, high school and college hockey player
When first looking for a power skating instructor I observed several male instructors I wanted my son to sign up with. When told by the skating rink that a female instructor was available I thought my son would reject that idea, due to wanting a male. He immediately said that's fine with him and we set up our first session. My son, Cole, finished the skating lesson and had the same reaction as I did—WOW, what a perfect fit. Kim pushes and encourages Cole with the perfect blend resulting in my son making his high school team, having never played ice hockey before. For my son to want to get up at five a.m. and skate with Kim says it all. She has shared her passion for, and knowledge of, skating with Cole who now wants to continue playing in college. Cole is a success story, thanks to Kim.

Richard Lucente, hockey father and adult student
As an adult who could barely manage to stand on ice skates, I became involved in a men's ice hockey league and picked up a game here and there. My experience was comparable to being in the bumper in a pinball game, having the great joy of watching my teammates score goals, while I had the occasional few. I could handle a check and recover, but that's about all I could do, given my skating ability. To my credit, I did occasionally get the

lucky goal which I claimed was a matter of skill rather than luck. I some-how continued to see myself as a good skater rather than a skater who had actual skills, which is why I was in need of help. Playing ice hockey was always on my top of my bucket list of lifelong goals, so I was determined to get to the point where I was that skater who scored a goal, not due to luck, but rather because I acquired the skill to do so. I was an adult skat-er who needed power skating skills rather than basic lessons. I consulted other hockey dads for a power skating coach since I am a father of a son who plays ice hockey. Unanimously, every hockey father pointed me in the direction of Kim. The next thing I knew, I was skating at six a.m. every Tuesday morning with the skating coach who is known to get anyone to the skill set they need.

My very first lesson with Kim was a measure of my ability, where she evaluated what skills I already had and skills that I needed to work on. Kim then quickly moved on and made a plan for what I needed to work on first, which included typical skills that every hockey player should know like the back of their hand. We worked on skills such as stopping, defense positions, and crossovers. I was bad, but Kim had nothing but encouraging words, making me feel that I could do nothing but improve. With each lesson, the focus was not on what I couldn't do, but things that I could work toward. Each session, I constantly felt that my skills and confidence on the ice were growing. She taught me that power skating was more than just physical endurance, it was a mental game as well, drawing comparisons from physics and famous skaters who overcome adversity to master the art of skating. Today, I continue taking lessons from Kim, but fortunately, I am a much safer skater and have a lot more confidence and fun when it comes to playing hockey. I look forward to the future as my ability contin-ues to grow. Many thanks to Kim Interdonato.

Gerry Broome, hockey coach and father of Tyler, high school hockey player
My son, Tyler, has been a student of Kim's since the fall of 2013. When I was looking for an instructor to teach my son how to skate, the choice was easy. I knew my son would respond well to a woman's touch. When Tyler first started to skate, he was a train wreck. After a few lessons, there was a noticeable difference. Kim not only taught Tyler, but she also took an interest in his skating needs. Kim and Tyler have formed a special bond. When Tyler scored his first goal, he made sure the first person he told was

Kim. Tyler is now an accomplished skater, and he has Kim to thank. He looks forward to each lesson and future lessons. Tyler and I are proud to call Kim a friend.

Thomas Pelio, father of TJ, travel hockey player
If you're looking for a skating coach to motivate your player with enough firmness to reel them in when their focus slips, Kim Interdonato is the coach for you. She brought my son to the next level quickly and continues to do so weekly. His edges, his stride, and his power have all turned the corner to the next level. She constantly maintained the balance of coach and mentor. My son is not only a better player because of her instruction, but he is a better teammate and person because of her.

Joe Densieski, father of Ryan and Matthew and hockey coach
I have twin boys, age eleven. My boys have been skating and playing hockey for eighteen months. With Kim Interdonato's help, their skating ability has improved an incredible amount. She taught them how to start, stop, balance, and use their edges. They have gone from barely being able to stand up to being the best skaters in their league. I would encourage anyone, young or old, to use a female power skating instructor like Kim to help increase their ability on the ice.

Sean Hopkins, father of Ryan, high school hockey player
My son, Ryan, is twelve years old and has been playing ice hockey for many years. He has become a very good skater, but in order to keep up with the speed and complexity of the sport, we decided to get him private skating lessons. We were lucky enough to find Kim, who changed Ryan from a good skater to a great one in a short amount of time. Kim not only goes through the drills in a methodical manner so that a student of any age can comprehend them, but she explains the reasons for the drills. Her coaching enables her to truly connect with her students, generating amazing results. Ryan looks forward to his lessons, knowing that each time he steps on the ice with Kim, he becomes a better skater. In just a few weeks, Kim was able to improve Ryan's skating technique and confidence which has resulted in his being a greater asset to his team.

Alexis Panagatos, female hockey student

Being a girl in ice hockey and having a female instructor in a male-dominated sport gives me confidence, inspires me, and gives me a sense of belonging. She inspires me by making me feel I can accomplish anything I want, even beyond playing in a male-dominated sport. I feel that if I had a male instructor, I would be looked down on and seen as weak and untalented. Having a female instructor makes me feel accepted. Having an instructor who is a female and loves hockey makes me feel capable of doing anything.

Georgia Halmo, figure skating for over fourteen years, Delaware College figure skating team

When you are coached by someone for fourteen years, you begin to view them more as family than anything else. Miss Kim has had my back for my entire life, and she was literally always there to pick me up if I fell down. I owe my passion for the sport and love of the ice to my first coach, Kim. Her cheery personality and happiness are contagious, and a lesson hardly goes by without laughs. Miss Kim cares deeply about her students, and I often feel she knows me better than I even know myself. Miss Kim has shaped me into the person and skater I am today, and for that, I am forever thankful.

Photo Gallery

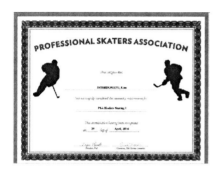
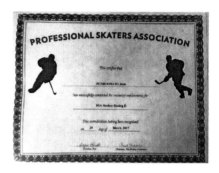

Me and Luke at age 3

*Me and Nick Kozlowski
(High-school Hockey)*

Kim teaching Cole Chamberlain

Kim teaching beginner

Andrew Morici high school hockey player

Evan Venth high school hockey player

TJ Pelio travel player

Paul Blase -Professional hockey player SPHL, Europe

Paul Blaze and Kim Interdonato after lessons

My son Luke Buck playing in his first travel game

Kim teaching Densieski twins (future high school hockey players)

Georgia Halmo (skating for the University of Delaware)
Gabby Castellano (figure skating while working on college degree)
Kim Interdonato PSA rated figure skating coach
Liz Robertson (competitive skater working towards Junior test)

NEVER GIVE UP

Let's face it, sometimes I do not want to wear the high heels or get dressed up. I just want to grab an old pair of my slippers and sweatpants and crawl up on the couch in a ball, engulfed by my electric blanket, only to watch mindless TV shows and eat vanilla frosting out of the container. Glad those days are few and far between.

Most days I love going to work, but I get to the point some days I want to fling my hockey skates off the bow of a boat. We all have those hard days, days where it takes every bit of our energy to get up and go. Being a power skating instructor is no different. Motivating myself to get to work can sometimes be a challenge. It is cold, and I am not in the mood to be Miss Sunshine, but then reality kicks in, and I change my attitude and usually have a great day.

There were several times I did want to give up my job. I even contemplated working for any company with benefits and a retirement plan. Figure skating was not paying the bills, and I just did not have that many lessons. Being on my own with a child was scary for me. It was a hard decision to make the move into power skating. I enjoyed the work, but changing my business over was not an easy task. Most everyone at the rink looked at me in a figure skating role. To this day I am still having to convince people the foundation I have learned while figure skating is strong and that's why I excel at teaching power skating.

The days I do not feel like not going to work are usually after a student dropped me for another instructor. My feelings get hurt, and my ego gets bruised. It is discouraging at times. It is hard not to take it personally but instead realize that it is part of the job. I get attached to students and always want to do my best. When they go to another instructor, I feel I did something wrong. But from time to time, things just do not click, or a student needs a change. They can benefit from another instructor. Then I try to think about the foundation I built for that student and focus on the greater good. What is best for the student? I am excellent at what I do, but not everyone is going to work well with my teaching style. That is my main focus. I never want to give up.

There are hours I want to spend with my son, family, and friends but I have to work. Then come those fun days on a Sunday, when I feel like everyone has the day off except me. I dread going to work on bright sunny beach days. I look out of the frozen glass as I am in layers of clothes at the people outside basking in the sun. I want to shed the jacket, long pants, and hockey skates for a cute, flowing sundress and heels. Eventually, I get off work and get my free time. I think, my students depend on me to be there and work as hard as they do, I never want to give up.

On cold dark winter's mornings, when the sun not rising for hours and the moon is still shining, I have to go out in the whipping wind to a frosted car to get to work, not being able to escape the chill. I really want to throw in the towel. The thought of getting out of my warm bed and dragging myself into a cold rink is awful. I head out armed with a hot cup of coffee, and once I am on the ice my core temperature adjusts, and it gets my body alive again. I still never want to give up.

As I get older, I have a few more aches and pains than I did the season before. I am not as fast as I once was. My knees get an unexplainable discomfort when I push down on edges that I was once proficient at performing easily. My body is letting me know the years are taking a toll. I do not want to complain to my students or show any sign of getting weaker. I cannot tell them to power through if I can't. As years pass by, it is inevitable that I am getting older, and I am not as strong as I once was. It can be extremely frustrating that my body is changing. And yet still I never want to give up.

I often wonder what the driving force is that makes me not want to give up. Sometimes I wonder if it is pride, wanting to be the best. Or could it be familiarity with being a skater for so long it is as natural as breathing? Could it be the fact that it's comfortable, that I do not know of a life without skating? I think I hit the lottery getting to do a job I love for so many years.

Most of all, I have my faith that things will always work out—faith that no matter what, if you want something bad enough in life you will achieve it. To be successful in anything you do, you need to have gratitude, faith, and the will to keep trying even when you think you're going to fail. I know for myself, my failures were the best lessons I ever learned. They continue to teach me to never give up.

CPSIA information can be obtained
at www.ICGtesting.com
Printed in the USA
FFOW02n1455250218
45232375-45819FF